D0948956

# A Firefighter's Tools

**Devon McKinney**

**PowerKiDS**
press.

New York

Published in 2016 by The Rosen Publishing Group, Inc.
29 East 21st Street, New York, NY 10010

First Edition

Editor: Caitie McAneney
Book Design: Reann Nye

Photo Credits: Cover (firefighter) Tetra Images/Getty Images; cover (background) Chantal de Bruijne/Shutterstock.com; pp. 4, 21 (ax) Kunertus/Shutterstock.com; p. 5 Surachai/Shutterstock.com; p. 7 Scott David Patterson/Shutterstock.com; pp. 8, 21 (hood, coat, gloves) Nikitin Victor/Shutterstock.com; p. 9 © iStockphoto.com/Oksana Struk; pp. 10, 21 (SCBA) tatajantra/Shutterstock.com; p. 11 Dale A Stork/Shutterstock.com; pp. 12, 21 (halligan tool) Uwe Bumann/Shutterstock.com; pp. 13,15, 21 (Jaws of Life) TFoxFoto/Shutterstock.com; pp. 14, 21 (hydrant wrench) artcphotos/Shutterstock.com; pp. 16, 21 (wedge) Louella938/Shutterstock.com; pp. 16, 21 (wire cutters) Deymos.HR/Shutterstock.com; p. 17 Fuse/Gettty Images; pp. 19, 21 (ladder truck) Keith Muratori/Shutterstock.com; pp. 20, 21 (rescue truck) Evok20/Shutterstock.com; p. 21 (flashlight) Brittny/Shutterstock.com; p. 21 (personal rescue rope) graja/Shutterstock.com; p. 21 (boots) L Barnwell/Shutterstock.com; p. 21 (carabiner) aperturesound/Shutterstock.com; p. 21 (pants) Flashon Studio/Shutterstock.com; p. 21 (hose) Phichai/Shutterstock.com; p. 21 (helmet) Chad McDermott/Shutterstock.com; p. 21 (hydrant) Christian Delbert/Shutterstock.com; p. 21 (extinguisher) dcwcreations/Shutterstock.com; p. 21 (fire engine) Matthew Strauss/Shutterstock.com; p. 22 Hero Images/Getty Images.

Cataloging-in-Publication Data

McKinney, Devon.
A firefighter's tools / by Devon McKinney.
p. cm. — (Community Helpers and their Tools)
Includes index.
ISBN 978-1-4994-0840-9 (pbk.)
ISBN 978-1-4994-0841-6 (6 pack)
ISBN 978-1-4994-0897-3 (library binding)
1. Fire extinction — Equipment and supplies — Juvenile literature. 2. Fire fighters — Juvenile literature. I. McKinney, Devon. II. Title.
TH9372.M43 2016
628.9'25—d23

Manufactured in the United States of America

CPSIA Compliance Information: Batch #WS15PK: For Further Information contact Rosen Publishing, New York, New York at 1-800-237-9932

# Contents

# Fighting Fires

Firefighters are community helpers who make it their job to save lives. They control fires and **rescue** people who are in danger. They fight small house fires and big forest fires. Firefighters also help with other **emergencies**, such as car crashes and **medical** troubles.

Firefighters use many tools to help them fight fires and stay safe. They wear **protective** clothing so they don't get burned. They also carry tools to help them break into buildings and save people.

## TOOL TIME!

An ax is often a **symbol** for firefighters. They use this tool to get into burning buildings to rescue people and pets.

Firefighters go through both live fire training and emergency medical training before they land their job.

# Bunker Gear

A firefighter needs to be ready to face high heat and huge flames. They need to wear special protective clothing, which is also called bunker gear or turnout gear.

Bunker gear includes a coat and pants that have many **layers** of cloth. The outer layer protects against heat and water. The inner layers keep the firefighter warm and dry. These clothes are heavy and big. However, they're loose and comfortable enough for the firefighter to move around easily.

## TOOL TIME!

Bunker gear is usually yellow or tan. Some gear has yellow stripes that catch the light. This makes the firefighter easier to see in dark and smoky surroundings.

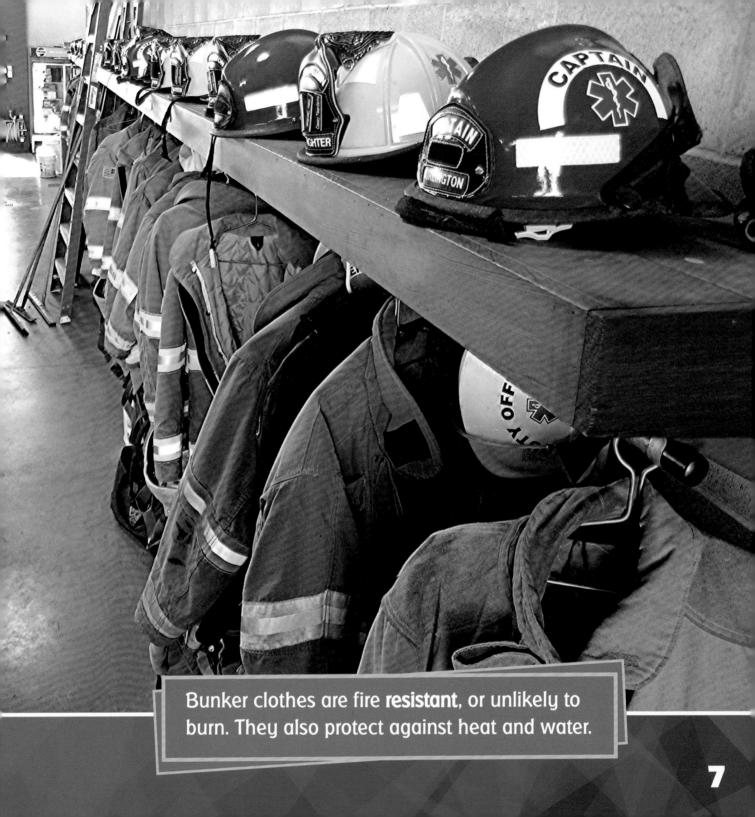

Bunker clothes are fire **resistant**, or unlikely to burn. They also protect against heat and water.

Firefighters need to keep every part of their body covered to stay safe from fire. They wear thick gloves on their hands. They also wear thick boots on their feet. Gloves and boots keep a firefighter's hands and feet safe as they enter a burning building or wildfire.

A firefighter's helmet is a very important tool. This hard hat protects the firefighter's head from falling objects. The firefighter also wears a fire-resistant hood around their neck, ears, and hair.

hood

## TOOL TIME!

A firefighter's hood should only leave enough of an opening on the face for a breathing mask. Every part of a firefighter's face must be covered.

The helmet has a **shield** to protect a firefighter's eyes.

# Breathing Easy

Walking into a burning building is unsafe for many reasons. Even if the flames don't touch a firefighter, the smoke can make it hard to breathe and harm their **lungs**.

Firefighters wear a special mask on their face and a tank of clean air on their back. The air is held in the tank until a firefighter needs it. Then, the air fills the mask so the firefighter can breathe clean air instead of smoke.

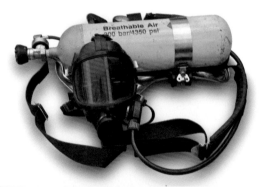

## TOOL TIME!

The mask and tank are part of one tool called a self-contained breathing apparatus (SCBA). An SCBA is usually worn like a backpack with straps to keep it on.

Like most of a firefighter's gear, their SCBA has to be fire resistant.

# Breaking In

Sometimes firefighters need to force themselves into a building or car. To do that, they use special tools. An ax can be used to break down doors, walls, and windows. It has a long handle and a flat, sharp head for breaking things.

A halligan tool has a long handle with two heads at the top. One is flat like an ax, while the other is sharp and pointed. On the other end of the handle is a claw to force things open.

halligan tool

## TOOL TIME!

Halligan tools can be used to twist, lift, hit, and cut things.

Firefighters use a tool called the Jaws of Life to rescue people from cars. Jaws of Life can easily cut through metal and make openings to get people out.

# Putting Out the Fire

Firefighters need special tools to put fires out. Sometimes, firefighters use **fire extinguishers** to put out a fire. Most times, firefighters use water. Where do they get the water?

Fire hydrants are firefighter tools you can find in every neighborhood. They're like big outdoor faucets, or taps, that get water from pipes under the ground. **Nozzles** on each side are covered by a piece of metal called a nut. A firefighter unscrews the nut and connects a hose to the nozzle.

## TOOL TIME!

A firefighter uses a hydrant wrench to turn a nut on top of the hydrant. This makes the water flow.

hydrant wrench

Fire hoses spray a strong stream of water on a building. They're very heavy, and it usually takes two or more firefighters to use one.

# Carrying Small Tools

While some firefighters spray water outside, other firefighters go into the burning building. They need to carry small tools with them in case of emergency.

Firefighters should carry a personal escape rope, which can be anywhere from 40 feet (12 m) to 300 feet (91 m) long. The rope should have a clip at the end called a carabiner. If a firefighter has to jump out of a building, they can clip the carabiner to something sturdy. Then, they can use the rope to climb down the building.

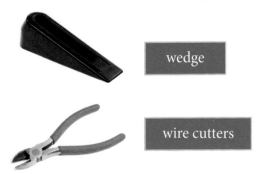

wedge

wire cutters

## TOOL TIME!

Other small tools firefighters should carry are a wedge and wire cutters. A wedge can keep a door open. Wire cutters can help the firefighter escape if they get tangled in something.

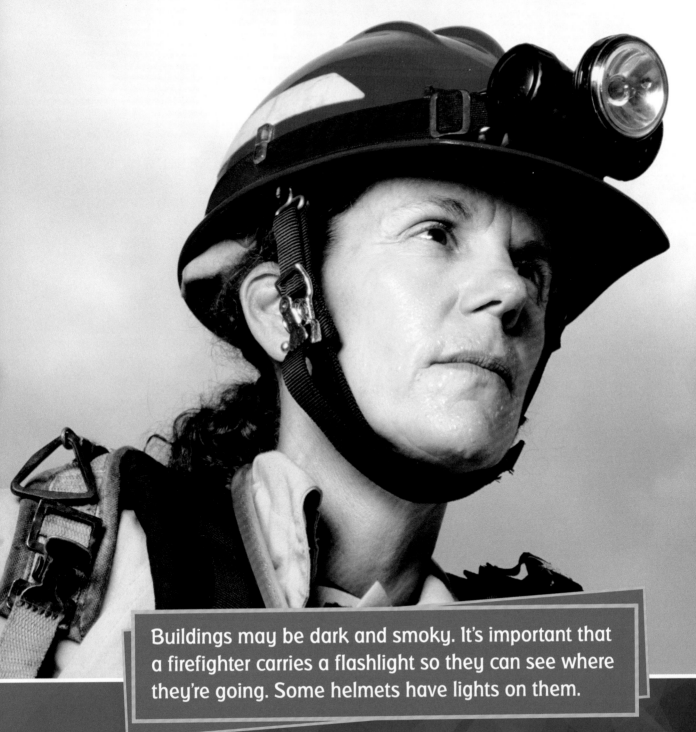

Buildings may be dark and smoky. It's important that a firefighter carries a flashlight so they can see where they're going. Some helmets have lights on them.

# Huge Trucks

Usually you hear a fire truck, or fire engine, before you see one. That's because fire engines have a siren, which is a device that makes a very loud sound. The siren warns other drivers that the fire engine is on its way to an emergency.

Fire engines carry firefighters to where they're needed. They have many tools on them, such as hoses, axes, and fire extinguishers. Some fire engines also hold a tank of water.

## TOOL TIME!

Ladder trucks carry tall ladders and other firefighting tools. The firefighters on these trucks sometimes save people from high windows.

ladder truck

fire engine

The firefighters who ride in the fire engine are in charge of getting the water and stopping the fire.

# Rescue Trucks

Not all firefighters arrive in fire engines to put out the fire. Some firefighters arrive in rescue trucks. They're responsible for helping people who are trapped, sick, or hurt.

Rescue trucks have many tools onboard. They have tools to help people who are trapped inside cars, such as the Jaws of Life and other hand tools. These trucks even carry rescue sleds and floating devices to help people stuck on ice or in water. They also have emergency medical tools.

## TOOL TIME!

Rescue firefighters might give oxygen, a gas we need to breathe, to people who have trouble breathing because of smoke. Some rescue teams even have oxygen masks for animals!

# A Firefighter's Tools

## What to Wear

coat

pants

boots

gloves

helmet

SCBA

hood

## Fighting Fires

fire hydrant

fire hose

hydrant wrench

fire extinguisher

## Small Tools

personal escape rope

carabiner

wedge

wire cutters

flashlight

## Trucks

fire engine

ladder truck

rescue truck

## Breaking into Buildings and Cars

ax

Jaws of Life

halligan tool

21

# The Future of Firefighting

New **technology** is on the rise to help firefighters save lives. **Sensors** in dry, hot places can see and smell fire so firefighters can stop the flames before the fire gets too big. A tool called WISPER can track a firefighter's location, body heat, and heartbeat and send the information back to their team. If a firefighter faints or loses their way, they can be rescued.

Firefighters rely on tools both big and small to help them rescue people from fires and other emergencies. With training, someday you could be a lifesaving firefighter!

# Glossary

**emergency:** An unexpected situation that needs quick action.

**fire extinguisher:** A metal tank filled with chemicals that can put out a fire.

**layer:** One thickness of something lying over or under another.

**lung:** A body part that takes in air when a person or animal breathes.

**medical:** Having to do with health care.

**nozzle:** A round tip at the end of a pipe, hose, or tube that creates a jet of liquid or gas.

**protective:** Keeping safe.

**rescue:** To free a person or thing from unsafe conditions.

**resistant:** Not harmed by something else.

**sensor:** A device that senses heat, light, motion, sound, or smells.

**shield:** Something that protects someone from something.

**symbol:** Something that stands for something else.

**technology:** The way people do something using tools and the tools that they use.

# Index

# Websites

Due to the changing nature of Internet links, PowerKids Press has developed an online list of websites related to the subject of this book. This site is updated regularly. Please use this link to access the list: www.powerkidslinks.com/cht/fire